FIDELITIES

For Linda
all the best
Liliane Welch
15-8-97

For Cyril

ACKNOWLEDGMENTS

Some of these poems have appeared or are to appear in their present form or in altered versions in the following publications: *The Amethyst Review, Les Cahiers Luxembourgeois, The Fiddlehead, The Nashwaak Review, The New Brunswick Reader, The Officers' Quarterly, On the Threshold: Writing for the 21st Century, Other Voices, Outreach, Parchment, The Pottersfield Portfolio, The Prairie Journal of Canadian Literature, The River Review, Tickle Ace, Tidepool, The Windsor Review.*

I am deeply grateful to Don Coles, Richard Lemm, William Proutey and Nic Weber for their friendship and editorial advice.

I also appreciate much the cheerful support of Ruth Miller and Ann Ward of the Mount Allison University Library.

Books by Liliane Welch

Poetry

Winter Songs (1977) chapbook
Syntax of Ferment (1979)
Assailing Beats (1979)
October Winds (1980)
Brush and Trunks (1981)
From the Songs of the Artisans (1983)
Unrest Bound (1985) chapbook
Manstorna: Life on the Mountain (1985)
Word-House of a Grandchild (1987)
A Taste for Words (1988) chapbook
Fire to the Looms Below (1990)
Life in Another Language (1992)
Von Menschen und Orten (1992)
Dream Museum (1995)

Literary Criticism

Emergence: Baudelaire, Mallarmé, Rimbaud (1973) with C. Welch
Address: Rimbaud, Mallarmé, Butor (1979) with C. Welch

Prose

Seismographs: Selected Essays and Reviews (1988)

FIDELITIES

by

Liliane Welch

Borealis Press
Ottawa, Canada
1997

Borealis/Tecumseh Press Limited
9 Ashburn Drive
Nepean, Ontario, Canada K2E 6N4

The Publisher gratefully acknowledges the financial support of the Ontario Arts Council.

Canadian Cataloguing in Publication Data

Welch, Liliane, 1937-
Fidelities

Poems.
ISBN 0-88887-165-1 (bound).—
ISBN 0-88887-167-8 (pbk.)

I. Title

PS8595.E54F49 1997 C811'.54 C97-9000031-9
PR9199.3.W416F53 1997

Cover: design by Bull's Eye Design, Ottawa; art by Harry Rabinger, *Terres Rouges - Esch/Alzette*, (1936, oil on canvas, 630 × 400 cm) Photograph of artwork by Gaston Rollinger

Photograph of author by Cyril Welch

Printed and bound in Canada.

Contents

I Where are the images

II The hot smell of wildflowers

III The point of January

IV Mirrors for the Athenians

V The past released and held

I. Where are the images

. . . the words fall lightly between us.

Eugenio Montale, *Two in Twilight*

Sunday Afternoons

Even today I dream the hush of Sunday afternoons.

My parents out for their weekly walk,
The stairway perfumed with plum tarts,
Or my room's window wide open to aloneness,
Teenage flights;
From three distant steeples decrees of bells,
Weekday routines unlocked
To indolence and God's shirts pinned
To backyard lines, flapping through our lives.
Though now that land is fugitive
From its Maker and throbs with
Cars, soot, and greed, and retreats
To sighs of ennui on the Seventh day.
Though now I travel the lagoons beneath
Cities of middle-age desires, cocktails
During happy hours, and radio plays—
More than the occasional sunrise of talk,
more than electric parties I love
stealing the fire of solitude.

Edens

I pictured America as paradise,
a gigantic meteor fallen from the future,
home to the soldiers who ended
the war and gave us children
chewing gum, and Switzerland was
also a garden of Eden
made by confectioners, its mountains
so many chocolate days of another life.
And France was a bazaar with peasant women
selling live rabbits and camembert.
I craved those places until it hurt
as they crowded into my scribblers,
prayers, or exploded all night
glowing round the room.
They stretched over my eyes,
buzzing like hallucinatory fairs.

And Luxembourg?
Crimson skies of a mining town, storm-tossed
steel arks with sirens, three churches
mounting guard with belfries and stained glass
eyes. Was it a stage-setting, a puppet show?
I startled into life there, year after year.

Churches and Wetlands

The teacher coaxed us
across the ocean and drew
America on the board in five colours,
huge rivers frothing around colossal rocks.
She claimed if American soldiers hadn't
freed us from the Germans
there'd be no more Luxembourg.
On May Day red flags
paraded by our school yard,
the party leaders
singing all labourers should
unite against big bosses,
even American ones.
"Down with capitalists!" they chanted,
hammers and sickles in their eyes.
In my room I'd be writing
to pen pals overseas and Tuesday
afternoons in the movies I rode
with cowboys into the sky.
I saved part of my pocket money
for a ticket to freedom.
On holidays my parents trotted in formal
dress up and down Main street;
they reckoned I studied at home while
I wrote to Sarah in California: *Europe*
bores me, a continent
plugged with churches and wetlands—

Here is a photo from our school excursion
to a medieval town up north.
I'm the girl in the knitted cap
emptying the days before I leave.

Maids in the 1940s

I always surrounded them with
a smell of ironing
starched linen
suitcases heavy with what
laughter leaves behind
or the cry of swallows swooping
july nights in northern skies

Their faces were clearings
after a day of rain through our street
past the lilac bushes behind iron railings
on hot
summer mornings
as we slept in

Their songs
pressed sadness out of
Europe's endless rain
they winter in my memory their
barrel-organ bodies
balanced precariously Sundays
on high-heeled shoes
strong hands locking the sun up behind
waxed floors, filled with loneliness

Loss

After the war when a motorbike
crushed her, my brother
lost a secret self. He wouldn't forget
Dora at the window, waiting patiently
for him after school, or yawning
discreetly while he talked with friends,
as he now does, tin in his hair,
under the linden trees of his childhood.
Half of a couple, Dora's dreams running
through his sleep, he has improvised
on solitude ever since.
He watches dogs zigzagging
ahead of their masters, dashing back,
terrified of losing
these other lives. Transfixed,
my brother waits until,
muzzle glued to the window, he can
chase with them through the cluttered
streets, the dread
of meeting that motorbike again.

Mines

I remember the mines' tunnels
those caves with red-layered night
staring from the hills
engulfing me on the photograph
dug from a box after house cleaning.

The mines were abandoned
clefts, a temptation
the priest warned about
carnal places
girls must be shielded from
all that red
underground, swirling
through veins, the sensuous
longing unabated, secret
strolls outside of town where
lips burn and the cool odours
rise again, indolent, insistent.

The young girl in a white dress
walks with a boy through the hills
toward the openings
their shafts wide-eyed.

Stories

Where are the old books
        that glittered each winter
evening during the war when everyone waited
        for freedom and how were the end of cold days
composed then with a story between shadows
        on the green strawberry wallpaper
a grandfather clock's tick and my mother
        on the button-leather sofa unwinding skeins
of wool from my wrists into bright balls or
        where are the legends open to other worlds and
the room with its old fashioned sewing-machine
        the repetitive lives of women adrift
amidst drowsy cats on sideboards the garden
        steaming outside asking us already
to leave that world behind

The Milliner

The milliner, old and weary—this Paris
evening in her shop—stares
forgotten at shoppers on the streets.
My mother's fingers,
adroit as hers once sewed
flowers across my winter bonnet.
And her eyes hooded like
my mother's wear an
intent frown, her fingers
gnarl like hers. My hands
twitch when she nods, her hats
blinking toward better times, frills
tied as the bright bows that once spilled
to the wind from my head. My mother's love
for me has vanished, caps
in some rag bag, her rebukes
in the wardrobe of my old room.
Now the milliner locks her door as my mother
used to, against a night so deep
she looks to passersby for deliverance.

All Saints

There was a mournful unease to the wind
when I stood amidst them.
We were strangers, cousins in name only
as we froze before the grave. I think now
we didn't fathom how sad those November
rituals were. First we heard mass in church.
Then we walked to the cemetery separated
by Latin prayers. All birds shut down.
We would sing: "Angels guide us
into paradise." Turned to the dead
whose faces stared afflicted from tombstones.
The priest wrapped in incense blessed us all.
No word to arrest death on those visits.
So that all my life I would map the wilderness
we shared whenever anyone said "family reunions".

Guides Then and Now

When I was five, during World War II, we made
angels in the snow on fields above
my home town shouting, *Paradise . . . paradise.*
Wings might save us from high black boots.
Today Eden seems for all my friends
shopping in malls, and flying above clouds
to Thailand. Meanwhile books and mountains
Convene my days. Two years after the war,
dressed as an angel in a church procession
my white-gold wings could swoop through heaven.
Since my youth, seraphs with muscular hands
have been blowing trumpets for resurrection,
while divine messages zoom to earth
for some few. And not long ago
Hoelderlin asked, *Why poets in times of need?*
Near Fundy Bay, my students say, Angels sleep
in Europe's locked cathedrals. And maybe therefore
I can walk here through the last light of paradise.

The Past

The path on which we track
our past is thinly marked,
beyond spruces, into green stillness
where the deer lie sleeping. Few trails
lead back, and there is
a deadly hush: although cries
have been heard, bodies
seen flash toward today's
brush. How to endure those ancient traces?
Some evenings we have locked
our doors, but the dark
never rests. It finds us
on the shores of sleep—
children, leaving
the heart of the woods,
warm blood on our hands.

Afterlife

As old people, we stand in its image.
A narrow-gauge red train will wait
and whistle repeatedly on the windy plains,
its compartments assorted: blue
upholstered first class, wooden-benched third.
Underway through tunnels, past torrents,
beyond the tree-line, over passes, our bearings
lost, near the mist-wreathed peaks of the afterlife,
we tremble giddy and awed, villages
perched on chasms still clinging to our eyes.

II. The hot smell of wildflowers

Today we take the great breath of lovers,
tomorrow fate shuts us in.

Ezra Pound, *Homage to Sextus Propertius*

After the War

It was after the war
When he became priest of a village
From the last century,
A tiny parish lost in the fog of the
Ardennes hills. As he
Stepped before the altar, God's eye
Would break through his cassock; he'd be
Master of that sweet kingdom
Where near a stained glass
Window I, his mother, could rest.
He'd pray, *Virgin Mary ...*
And I'd think of our meal,
Roast duck, a fine bottle of Bourgogne
After mass. He'd let his hand
Stroke the embroidered flaps
Of the cobalt blue stola
I had ironed and laid out for him
Caressing the folds in the garment;
The candlelight and incense round
The old ladies they'd sing, *Mary, chaste Queen*
Thrill us with patience ...
And bow as he blessed their marriage
To solitude. One day a school teacher
Arrived, a young woman—
From the city she brought
shiny high-heeled shoes;
When she entered the church,
All the old farmers turned their heads.
She'd stare at the pulpit, long for some
Other heaven, murmuring, *Hail Mary ...*
Be our intercessor ...
And her bright dress would burn
His eyes. My son
Always bashful. This saintly man
And that impure creature?

He had to be protected.
She visited the parsonage
For confession, wearing
The silk hose I envied
Up a long slit in her skirt.
Once, peeking through the crack
Of his study's door I saw that
Arm encircled with bracelets,
That hand grab his knee. She owned
Up to the darkness inside her soul.
And I heard her say, *Father, why has*
God exiled us in grace's monotony?—
Bending forward, she bared her teeth,
Flashing her eyes at his holy face.
And said, *Father, sometimes I hunger*
To be the sin that Our Lord uses
To kill false saints ...
Later, as I stood with my clean apron outside,
She rushed up to me,
Her clothes flapping perfume.
Rocking before the Virgin's shrine
She let out a cry, *Where's the solace*
For you or me?

Man of God

I stalk the orchards of paradise,
where sundrawn apple trees leave damp ground
for divine plans. In my prayers
I see gardeners and saints meeting
under the pergola of lascivious talk.

This morning, the sky whirs with sin,
the flowers pungent, the beasts cocooned by temptation.
I question Lucifer about the Gospels,
and at once the wine is so
full-bodied it sends me to the snowfield

of the altar, and suddenly the statues
hold their breath and wild desire climbs out of
a woman's mouth confiding,
I am a summer flower, you are my bee.

And so I enter the confessional
the woman's words are scarlet kisses.
The crowded dark burns me. God,
why are you silent again?

The Last Show

He creates his face colour
by colour, daring each bright
shade to dilate hushed surprise.
A white forehead releases
the wonder of new snow, and black lines
open the eyes onto midnight.
Burgundy rouge and autumn purple
fire the cheeks. Yellows conjure
the laughter of dawn. He winks at the mirror
as the owner sells the circus, impatient
with empty seats, anxious
to redraw his life, settle
in one place. The clown forgets all this
as he dips his fingers into the paint,
feeling his mask widen
applause, the make-up
he'll have to throw away.

Still Life

After he turned seventy and lost the race,
he disassembled and cleaned his racing bike
on a sheet spread over the living room
floor, a still life from surrealist times,

then hung the bicycle under the roof
wrapped in a yellowing dress, next to
his skis stored inside trouser legs,
then pulled from a shoe carton

the newspaper cuts about his racing,
his skiing meets, carefully
stuffed these trophies into an envelope
and addressed it to his unborn grandson.

Marriage

Moonlight: a fisherman kneeling near his boat.
They've been married long and he hovers
round the curves of its hull. Still stroking
it. Remembering how he loved its privacy,
when the radio said: "Our fishery is dead."
He looks at the sea, the fine curtain
of fog they used to traverse at dawn,
the early sheen that the sun enters, that
only true travelers adore. Restless flight
of whitecaps. Downpour of light,
wind on his face, the mind's speed
increases. Far out, today's salt.

Immigrant

Even in the steel mill, his home land held him,
even as he toiled, with fiery rods;
the lime-scented evenings on hot piazzas,
the dark-eyed espresso, his mother.
Even as he slaved, stubbornly, as only immigrants
can slave, fiercely, Italy
impinged, blotted out the forge's grip.

The bustling streets with their ochre palazzi
supplanted the whistle's blows;
and even pardon flowed from his mother,
who had never lived immigration,
only bambini, kitchen, church.

At night, Italy moved elsewhere and nowhere:
abandoned the smokestacks when he lay
hungover from work,
making room for the misty northern forests,
fleeting bliss with blond women.

Only an Italian

His weekdays were sweat, his Sundays
card games—a man married
to red night
underground. He was only
an Italian, there
in Esch, and it was only early
this century—the rise
of Luxembourg shaped
by bent spines. Erased name,
effaced voice, the loneliness
in his eyes forgotten today,
a life vanished. For
forty years his hands
reaped the mine's rock.

Artist's Husband

Art exhausts him, he longs
to escape from it: trips to museums,
and exhibitions, artsy talk,
his wife's bohemian friends and tastes.
He burns to live in the future,
forgetting portraits by masters.
He wants to traffic
with guns, finger their bolts,
pull triggers, palm bullets.
Computers mesmerize him, alone at night
his eyes caress their screens. He revels in
scientific journals, reason's cult
is his book of days. She
has always needed him, first
as lifeboat, salvation from parents
smothering her talents and then as
loyal consort for thirty years. Now
she paints in the studio, hearing
downstairs his installation
of a fax machine, his thoughts
slanted like those of a master
ignoring the primitive
tribes he has subdued. She knows that
despite her many prizes, always
he'll judge her art feeble and inferior,
a vestige from vanished years.

Siegfried and Melusine in 1994

In a gourmet palace
on Luxembourg's narrow streets,
a savory intimacy
bridged the black-tie night,

and rich-smelling wisdom
of ancient chefs banned guests
grazing on mere snacks.
The chic heiress

with toffee hair, cognac
in hand felt at home.
Here he courted
her to open up,

but she withdrew coyly, guarded
her riches from his clever probes.
Serene on this Saturday,
fastidious, seductive,

she would not be
one of his rainbows.
Maybe her heart was
a well without gold,

and he—a dizzy
sensualist of banknotes,
race cars, and caviar—
feasted on denial.

That winter he was not
amorously aligned with
other wealthy women:
only with whores, nuns, props.

Anniversary

That winter night in Bruges,
Walking through the snowy streets
Lit by shop windows and ancient lamps,

A Flemish girl approached him—
A Sibyl from the Memling painting
He had studied, her pewter eyes piercing

Like his wife's—Later, at his hotel
Malcontented, worn out—he paced
Through his love museum, swaggered

Past demons in low-cut dresses, longing
Nailed to the walls. The pink unctuous
Perfume of his last mistress, all heavy

With messages; autumn-eyes rolling back
Eros' tombstone. He shivered in the cold
Weather that had engulfed him

During those years he lay in so many beds ...
Then remembered
That winter night had been the anniversary,

His wife's departure igniting all this.

Rebound Lover

Why had he left Toronto for the provinces?
Did he want to trade sinlit cities for skiing
From his backdoor into endless woods?
Was New Brunswick a rebound lover for vacant souls? ...
No, his New Brunswick, with its history of defeats,
Had consoled so many falls,
In its quiet he ran down the steps of sentences
Without looking back—beyond the tired dominion
Of lies, futilities, blank smiles.

One morning Dawn appeared early
At his house.—As he ate breakfast, he watched
Her high cheekbones lit by anger ... And she
Pulled a chair close to him, her lips pushing out
Haloes of cigarette smoke, as she raged, "I hate
Your face, your parties and guru friends.
Loving you is like being a mannequin.
Queen Elizabeth has more privacy.
One more thing: I refuse to clean
Your mirrors anymore, try a blind woman."
He heard doors slam, an affair like a train car
Smoothly glide away, pathos everywhere.

Ten years later, he saw Dawn's slender back
In Montreal, moving through the door of a boutique,
—the way a huntress guides her horse
Through felled maples, intent, arousal in the air ...
He continued his stroll. Then remembered a dark and icy
Night, walking through snowbanks, kissing her long neck
Between a fox fur collar, as they approached
The luminous windows behind which she sat
In a portrait with her children above the mantle;
Hope-tinted desire shining through ...
Both of them moving stealthily as thieves. Outside
Then always ... Into the hinterlands of deceit.

Wildflower

Clothes her beatitude.
Frocks and the soft labyrinth her wardrobe contained.
All the costumes were her selves, though not one ever was.
And what she wore that fall, her fox coat hinting escape.
It translated me to a train ride one afternoon
When sun stamped her shadow through windows,
Along birches and spruce, rock escarpments, and suddenly
upright
Over a wooden barn. She was here and not here,
Up close and again far away. The fox searching
For the heart. Now the wardrobe—
With that fur coat from Norway and her gowns—stands empty;
How to hold a woman against perdition.
Sometimes such questions dart like birds inside.

Once she returned from her wardrobe in the dark.
All day I had lusted for her, stripped
At last, without the endless disguises.
I lay on my side, she slipped under the sheets.
She wore a transparent chemise embroidered with wildflowers,
And she resumed her week long crusade
For a blouse that left me with the longing
Of the Trappists at Orval. Today their abbey
Is a tourist attraction, prayers departed or fallen asleep,

But one May we ambled through the ruins
And the shop where earnest men sell cheese and beer.
Holy images and postcards and games for children. "Victuals
That lodge God in body and soul," as the monk told us.
He stared at her tanned legs blazing
Out of tight red shorts. "Taste this.
We've made it for centuries, and thrived."
Next to me in bed the hot smell of wildflowers
invaded. Alone now, what can I borrow
from the wardrobe on cold nights?

III. The point of January

My desk, most loyal friend.

Marina Tsvetaeva, *Desk*

Winter Fires

At the point of January
That juts farthest into Siberia,
Our living room of fires and baroque music, we sit,
Reading and talking with the travelers
Trekking through the novel to Nepal.
On the wall: Knaff's oil painting
"Winter Fires," torches and matchsticks, fireplace
And cones. They crackle loud,
Sparkling through our windows into the forest
Where we walk over ice-crusts, where
One squirrel ignores wind and storm and
Fiercely tears spruce tips for survival.
Old World people would avoid
This habitat, locked in ice.
And why should they prefer to leave
Europe's cities, culture's laureated snort?
Why come to these woods, where hinterlanders
Study winter fires with leisurely passion?
We listen to violin partitas, imagining the warm
Colours filling a church . . .
Just as we turn a page our heroes scale
Black rock, hearing the silence of frozen streams.
Logs turn crimson and flick
Purple tongues. We move closer.
And the blasts of the blizzard
Against the house are lions, are
Gladiators running blinded
Through the underground passageways into the sun.

Dwelling

How many houses have I entered
where intense conversation, and love of books,
and peaceful hours set aside for writing
transform us, as we leave that everyday
when we're uncertain how to go on: hungry and nervous,
or worshipping transient gods,
or violating trust, thinking that we need
forget dwelling, or like adolescents,
earphones on the head, who for years are obstinate
and turn the music up, and already are deaf.
We wear our nights inside—effigies
of grandparents, and companions
who desired and urged and recalled,
the friend who carried his ladder over shale
listening to the wind between the rungs,
the woman who flowed into her man like a river,
vanished, and never reappeared. Could they
help me inhabit silent afternoons,
when all alone, I bring in my thoughts from the line
outside, to answer a letter, and toward evening
my lover comes to cook a meal, the smell of bread
drifting into the bedroom until we fall asleep?

Ron

Ron, a poet I met ten years ago,
Who once traveled to Paris
With me for a poetry festival—
Then spent the noon hour jogging
In the Tuileries Gardens, where
An old French bum watching him
Run by, called out
"That's merely bricolage, Monsieur,"
While Ron was already soaring in mind
Through next month's Montreal marathon,
The contenders high on new scores, the city
Less regal than ancient Paris—Ron,
Telephoned today to review his triathlon scores,
And with gregarious charm began
Proselytizing about health clubs to lure me
From my confinement into sport cults,
Odysseys without end . . .
Then Ron praised the new gym next door,
A cathedral, an anti-chamber to paradise,
Where you worked out on the Nautilus,
Progressed to stationary bikes, perspired
Through T-shirt, headband and Walkman,
Then slipped into the steam bath,
Ended on top of the world with a massage.
There were mysterious prayers,
In the muscles as you loped exhausted
Back to salvation in the locker room.
And now, he reported, ten mile runs at dawn
Were visits to a museum,
The fall maples bursting into a fire of reds,
A heat you could penetrate only with eyes
Drastically rewired. Just yesterday
Such flames overwhelmed him that he became
A Chagall canvas, so he proposed:
A joint celebration of body and soul

As together we'd found a retreat on Deer Island,
A gateway to ultimate fitness. Ron,
Whose exuberance could reroute rivers,
Was at the moment, he admitted,
In a dry period with his writing,
And would teach a composition course
Mainly to finance a new racing bike,
And as he mused about bodies not breathing,
Poems rippling lazily, he exploded:
"I never had a talent for monogamy!"

Girl Passing in Sackville

The way Baudelaire spotted a passing
Mysterious mourner draw close her grief,
A black embroidered hem
Clasped as an amulet against roaring
Paris, deafening demons, lightning it struck
Until her eyes bonded him
To an eternity where joy can kill;
So I met her sister
Friday night on Sackville's four-way corner
Amidst traffic hiss and exhaust, lithe
Figure, accomplice of darkness and
A swarming street. Flowers of
Evil from the night.
Moved by me. A flash,
A longing. The flicker
Of her gaze, a small town's cry.

Accomplice

Pens: most with visible ink chambers
(Children we rejoiced, "Now we're grown up"),
Inkwells abandoned, stained glass windows
Gleaming in our hands. I treasured them all,
Those dark wands stringing barefoot
Words on white pastures.
Yet, there's one, faithful accomplice
On two continents for over thirty years.
My Mont Blanc pen, black with a white star,
Feels cool to the touch as a marble scepter
Full of hidden light—the sun's last infusion.
What I dared not utter or do
Lives in this pen: My backpack still
Waits to be carried up the Mont Blanc—
I ascended other legends, and peaks, so
Mountain climbing became a postscript
To writing. Today, while
A friend will cross the Alps
On skies, swerving hieroglyphs
Down powder snow, I pause
At my desk, ink stains my fingers,
The pen sees what I did not.

Together

I never thought the mountains would last
through old age. Or if they did
they'd backdrop a black and white film.
Now they come to me
as sedimentary dreams. I climb
the Matterhorn. Its name's ice. Juts
into a broken piece of sky. I walk
over cloudbanks into stillness,
the sun's speechless, up there,
a granite blue. Casts longing glances
down the valley. Dips into meadows,
is reborn as fireweed. I finally know
how to descend.

A Postcard

We study the symmetries
of Zermatt: men
in bright shirts carry
little children carefully
on their backs up the paths;
young chamber maids,
like spring suns, appear
for a moment behind windows
piled high with eiderdowns,
and the summer
has stopped here to pick
me up. At the alpine museum
this afternoon we recalled
the mortality of courage.
Toward evening, in silent glisten
the Matterhorn—
a house on fire
roofed with pink smoke—
is lapped at
by southern winds.

Foxes

Enjoy the land, wrote Thoreau,
but own it not—
he was a fox. Like
insects or children, Thoreau
possessed heaven.

Some foxes find pleasure
belonging to the ground:
poets, musicians,
some mountain climbers. And
my partner whom I suspect to be
a fox in hedgehog disguise.

Real foxes: fireflies,
tiny lighthouses of summer
nights. Cupped hands closed
on one such gem
was a triumph in childhood.

Flea Markets

On Sundays my friends free of their families
browse the flea markets and escape
their own silences—how boring for the men
left behind. Scattered trinkets, remains
strewn over tables.

Was that bracelet fastened to a girl's wrist
by a lover's hand? Does this music box
contain the ardour of a lady who furnished
her ennui with the Sugar Plum Fairy's Dance
from *The Nutcracker Suite*? Bought,
possessed, would these blush or blaze
at home?

Monday mornings, hung over from browsing,
my friends cross miles of business to bring
intimacy to their men. The flea markets
they carefully conceal behind telephone talk.

Summer

Deep in the Ardennes,
A summer of shorelines and suns, we lingered,
Removing our clothes and slowing the day.
In the months ahead: winter's
Solitude, winds and echoes,
Bright glassy rooms. I'll see you
Swimming across the lake below
Cliffs in mid-August when
The sky's furnace is pouring light
Onto your back, a buoy
Moored to fire, just as I'm held
By frescoes of angels flying into Nativity
Scenes. Before diving into the lake to swim
Back, you waved, a slender god,
Incarnate of every body signalling summer's
Epiphany. I swam out to meet you.
And together our arms cut the warm waves.

Titles to be Announced

They’re lying under students’ beds
or hidden behind the radiator
of some apartment, waiting to be freed—

ageless volumes in which writers
reside with aches in their heads,
having spent their eyes for others.
Or there are those

trapped as ghosts inside old-timers,
tapping to be remembered,
anxious for a reader who craves
a book that will lead him
through apple orchards elsewhere.

Birthday

The rain falls softly through me this late
October morning. Washes
what I've surrendered to or forgotten.
Letters about the death of friends. Dresses
turned yellow in closets, not thrown away.
Conversations each dawn with ancient rocks.
An immigrant's life. Februarys
poppies lighting the sky. Julys
housed by ice, fleeing the sun's whip.
The rain shared my epiphanies.   In Switzerland
on Piz Badile. In Bruges near dark canals.
At cafés with men, amid earnest thoughts.
Now the rain gives a Sabbath
to this fifty-eighth return of my birth.

Tourists

En route to warmer grounds the snow geese
pause in Fundy's marshes—
a grey whirlwind striding like priests
through Rome, panning dark pools
for roots they swallow whole,
tourists living it up.

They inspect brown grass, tethered to loam,
clustered weeds. Bull reeds
leashed by water, look
south. An aboideau
locks in first frosts. Their long necks strain.

Tides already cross winter benchmarks
on the dikes. November stacks
its ice cushions, soon they'll descend
on us, hunters with dogs.
The birds will be gathered
like praying nuns.

The slate sky is quick to vault down.
As first storms approach the geese
prepare their launch. Above the bark
of north winds, they hear another music.

Desire

Lemon trees grow in the heart,
She said
about her youth elsewhere.
They sometimes do here, wafting their odours
Into wool coats.

Late October, near Fundy Bay,
Autumn blushing through cat-tails,
My door searched now by spying winds,
Bronze light sweeping abandoned marsh grass.

Silent, still free from snow, woods wait
For hunters to enter their brush
with heavy boots
As the game wakes into wildness.

Her words stake my life down.
Under Sicily's sky,
all winter,
She ran through the lemon trees,
Expecting corridors of blooms.

I await July, that blazing grove.

Our Woods

At this edge, they turn
their back on the world, trap
burnt out campfires, hidden
paths. They thrive on

winters with ice-pennants,
moody springs,
summers of green rain,
blood coloured falls.

Churches, eateries move up to
them, let them know they're not
abandoned, that happiness is
the food you haven't tasted yet.

But the woods stretch a thousand
miles beyond fingers and mouths,
into morning silence, journey
to grounds unknown.

Maritime Skies

You drive into them on the Trans-Canada,
huge yachts skimming spruce woods,
their white sails roused by restless winds,
or vertical ladders grey
as granite, perfect for climbing—

Maritime skies where
many faces swell and snap
when circling the sun's shadow
pressed by distant horizons, anxious
for other lives. Or those

clouds at sunset navigating fields of wild
lupine, witness to miles of loves,
young women with pink finery who come
laughing and talking until dark
to find their place in our days,

a sky for which you must raise
your eyes off the road, yet that pours
the finest brandies, wines
from prisms beyond the headlights
while you speed silently into the night.

IV. Mirrors for the Athenians

Night sometimes brings to life
an unusual plant.

Francis Ponge, *The Candle*

Tattoo

After the war she could live
only *Auschwitz*, sitting with relatives
in their sunlit kitchen, her immortal
rock. And when she ate the chocolate
cake and picked up all the crumbs,
it was always *Auschwitz*, a new disbelief,
maybe, or the cell blocks now
bolted, like the soot sky,
the tiered bunks a watermark
left intact inside her head. Each sip
of coffee in the china cup,
a fresh flow of grief
she'd shouldered, had been
miraculously freed from, but now
it was everything, the dress
she pulled tight around her hips,
black comb in her hair, nephews
when they turned cartwheels,
all cast down the mass grave
of that word. And in dreams
she sang it, dark lullaby
as she strained
to wake, cradling,
her tattooed arm
like a lost child.

Mirrors

Why is the classroom her true place?
She has been teaching students for thirty years
and still is besotted by the swiftness of their
impatience. She still follows their gaze
out the window, tracking thoughts dry and
pungent as wildflowers. Why did she want to keep
the young awake? She relished standing
on the edge of knowing she did not know.
Like a swimmer slipping lightly into the water,
the river familiar but undeciphered.
Socrates before his death erected
one last time mirrors for the Athenians
to view themselves and the Mediterranean
sunlight.

Envy

Yes, she imagines her colleague
owning a villa in Provence
with a swimming pool lined
by cypresses—she fabulates more.
Chews this delicious fruit
through long winters. Sleeping
and waking she walks
a maze, his thrilling
summers and women
blight the secret paths,
gnawing betrayals.
Why can't she escape each spring
from these somber skies,
come back each fall, her hair
full of gold, why is she
trapped and he lured
by women with French haircuts
and shoes? Now her silent
rituals rehearse death
near a swimming pool with cypresses,
she buries her head in a book
to drown out passion's bickering,
and as for the resolve to undo him
when he returns, she'll turn to stone.
Or she will offer herself again.

Belgian Winters

Pinning wash on the line, she flies
to the Brussels in December when she was young,
composing love letters: To a Russian prince?
Did her words kiss that icon? Swallow the world?
Want to die of this sweetness?
She lived as if strolling through an ancient
forgotten library, bookshelves became
streets in St. Petersburg, where
red-faced men play cards,
kerchieved women bend over stoves,
and children dream after tugboats
moving down river toward the Baltic.
The house filled with labyrinths of
Russian prose, novels in which
her mother often escaped housework,
rushing through courtyards to meet
fur-coated lovers, her literary adultery
a blush over wintry Belgium.
Handkerchieves dance with the wind,
the mother's longing in the daughter's hands.

Mornings at Home

She saw stones fly through the sky.
    They'd eat fruit on Alsatian
Plates, when in late
    Spring, through the glass doors,
She'd see in the meadow two horses
    Nip at each other;
She'd look at her husband over the teak table
    Then out to the woods
Where the early blackbirds
    Were exchanging night for day.
She'd always crave honey,
    Wondering about mens'occupations ...
With him at work long days,
    Entering computer screens,
Forgetting her, at home lost in books.
    She'd amble through them,
Their church light awakening
    The angel lost in her body—
Austere, seignorial, the bread winner,
    He'd prepare to leave as she remained,
Standing within her life, clearing
    The table, waiting for him;
He'd gaze at her thinking, children
    Will redirect that exasperation ...
Each morning, closing the door behind him,
    She'd sit down stroking a book
Before cleaning the bathroom
    Floor. Thinking how on the threshold
Smiling, he always patted her head.

Smell of Fresh Bread

Conspiring with freedom
on powerless afternoons, she presses
her hands to the table,
kneading dough.

Into its warmth she sinks,
away from dead years, lost rooms.
Until the oven gleams
as a parachute and the house
fills with the smell of fresh bread.

Dream Land

She touches the pearls and the perfume phials
On her vanity. They shimmer with
Beaches or nights invented
By Narcissus,
These feral masks of herself, and lurk
Behind the moody calm
On fog-locked days, or the bustle
Of department stores. They are messengers
When they flash at dusk,
Bringing her closer
To pleasures obscured in this stained north,
Don't they? Meanwhile on the black vanity
Her hands grope toward a life
Charged by the sensual
Ceremonies of her dream land:
Florida.

Architecture of Retreat

On a dresser the tiniest Chinese box houses now
her life, slipped inside others larger, brighter.
She loves how this intimate boudoir
engraves her emptiness. As though truth
were more visible with each retreat toward the inside.
Her small steps kindle
the smoldering stove under her dress
as the first flurries of sleet traverse each box.
She discards silk stockings, elegant gloves,
scented scarves. When her hands
grow stiff she ponders why the dark
penultimate space has lost
its glitter and becomes
remote. Is it neglect or discontent
that freezes her into the hypnotic gaze
of a Byzantine mosaic all alone?

Contessa

She enters the afternoon
latticed by perfume.
Ancient, regal and fragile.
Admirers departed or dead.
And possessions, the crystal flasks
she so prized now only heirlooms:
shattered or stolen.
Fatigue increasingly her consort.
Clutching jewels and photographs
to not be commandeered.
Each day rewriting
her will. Tucked in her salon,
waving away the casual
advent of insight.

V. The past released and held

Their ancient, glittering eyes were gay.

W. B. Yeats, *Lapis Lazuli*

Relief

She is dying of old age. Her ancient cities are museums,
and her citizens perplexed. Abandoned by the gift
of surprise and change. Still Europe hangs on
talking to herself. But not for relief.
Not even to outlive death. She goes on because
she believes in ruins. She fabulates about two young
nuns from the New England woods.
How they come to Rome each summer, hungry
and in lay clothes. The cardinals dread
every year their invasion of the Holy City,
alert, for centuries, to ennui
inhabited now by a lonely
God. Discontented, walled in doubt
they turn their faces away. Contemplate
how the nuns' carefree prayers will find
deceit under marble floors.

Unfinished Painting

We walked into France, over fields
heavy with wheat, larks singing,
as in a Klopp tableau,
past nailed portals, farm houses,
billowing sheets. Crossed the Moselle
on a bridge drawn
by this Magus. Blue, green meadows,
tranquility carved from the breeze.
We reached fortified Sierck,
where pilgrims pray to the Virgin
for new faces, where ancient light tempts.
The Marienfloss shrine waits beyond
suspended walls, a canvas unfinished.
Perhaps he never knew
how the Madonna hides
behind shadows and vows.
Noon spilled mustard scent. Church bells
rang each hour through our steps.
We let Klopp finish his painting.
The Moselle blurred, shimmered.

46, rue Hippolyte-Maindron

At dawn outside the Parisian
workshop, a thrush in the tree,
opens his topcoat
to sing, tuning the sculptor's ear
and icons with salvos of joy.

The leaves are concert hall for that musician,
always the sky is lit yellow,
Paris posing as jungle,
whet mud to be shaped.

Always
Giacometti alone with the bird
I don't know who I am nor what I'm doing
... and those matchsticks dispersed
battleships on a grey ocean
he writes down.

The Cat

At night, when cafés open their doors
when Giacometti leaves his brush
on the easel's rim,
the cat pulls on its boots
struts out, and joins
the vagabonds, in their vesperal rites.

And Giacometti, intent
over a café table, thinks
of destroying a Rembrandt
at the Louvre
to free a trapped cat, or
of saving without hesitation
the cat
would his atelier burn down . . .

Nude with Head

When the head
rides away
from a torso
it thaws the ice
on our eyes,
the warmth
in gestures,
the magic
of fragrant
skin
or the cries
so tense
we hear them
at the mind's edge.

Ah! those undressed
curves are a mirror
of privacy's small fires—
the head must desire
awakeness
in flesh
to let the body's windows
fill with light.

Visiting Lotar in Stampa

Lotar greets me like a landscape,
darkness its flare.
If I were a sculptor I'd carve mystery
from a lover's eye. A northerner I'm friend to
polished stones, those gathered
while hiking down moraines, those
deflecting winds. In Stampa's
museum I visit Giacometti's
Lotar, a man crouched
on the knees. His lean body
translates rocky sainthood.
If I were an artist I'd erect
a curtain of images before whoever
migrates between valley and peak.
Images with the fragrance
of gardens on summer nights.
Lotar's blackness needles my hands.
Does he need me to shape his light?

The Dog

One day I saw myself in the street
just like that. I was the dog.

The snout scans below
while its long paws push
upward the curved hunger
that impels it to seek a home.
When it roves by
I stalk it, but there
on the bronze sidewalk
where the dog persists
stands Giacometti
—vagabond cartographer—
and with starved eyes
he searches the dark,
asks if I would also be
that dog.

Fidelity: Colville's "Dog and Groom"

He kneels intently on the red tiles smoothing
the bright pelt, as he does every morning
before the fireplace. His bond grows deeper
with each stroke. He recalls
when the golden dog came into his life.
The house had been silent for months.
She followed him, and now she stands tranced;
incarnate of every dog. Her face locks us into
her eyes. Two liquid brown stones are
the faint cello sound of the heart. His hand loses
itself in the fur. Animals bear no malice,
but an innocence promised, a fidelity forever
renewed. It is raining when he stops grooming,
the windows alive with light drumming.
This afternoon he will be in his studio, claimed
by the dog's presence. Painting the glad silence
inching from the paws into his hands.

The Angel Speaks:

In the Hans Memling year 1994

While you wintered up north, you envisioned me
singing with other angels
in a Flemish painting at Bruges. I must correct
you about angelic faith.
Figure me daring to fly out from
my canvas. Or, if I am to stay, ponder
the vacant days, the fantasies that assail me
come February, when Fundy Bay is under
ice and snow. That, your land, you must praise: yet,
I want to share your meals, your thoughts
like grace giving me a hearth, and my loneliness
shielded by your gaze. Can you ever
picture how angels endure a museum's
empty rooms. If you believe
the city of poetry never going dark,
can you imagine
traveling through doubt, stranded at midnight,
our hymns cold embers in the wind
even before seduction and sin: I bear
the ancient torment of light.

Holland

It was a beach like the movie
I saw one afternoon in Luxembourg,
Memory's huge hull receding through the mist.
We strolled over dunes rolled
High above the surf, past lighthouses.
Families riding black bicycles
Into miles of sunbeams at low tide.
On white sands an old man made love to a young girl.
As we waded through tidepools
The clouds tricked us into old tableaus,
Unfolding an ordered world.
We sailed to those urgencies
Only paintings can hold. Into the dark
Of an evening school, sleet sweeping
The roofs outside, while two candles lifted
The shadows from a boy's wobbly hand
On a slate and a girl's intent finger
Deciphering words, as ice shut down January.
Like those students we consented to travel,
To renewal, the art fetishes of some low land.

Household Tools

The 1996 Johannes Vermeer Exposition

We walk into these
    paintings, an intimate
little street, through passageways
    the inner courtyards
of quotidian concerns.

Stories sealed
    by the hourglass
of silence. How intense
    their lives are,
resonant, serene. This figure,

Vermeer's milkmaid, raising
    her red arms
over odour of bread,
    to pour milk.
Let's prolong that light.

The century of discovery.
    A woman gazing into her
mirror, a writer
    transfixing her viewer,
a geographer searching the outside.

Faces charged by bridled desire.
    Can we grow those eyes?
And the milk keeps flowing from
    strong hands, stained as sunsets,
handling household tools, making
    everything possible.

Poet's Grave

A homeless life.
Prague he carried through Europe.
Old city squares, baroque churches, fortresses on hills were stage sets for failed plays.
Guest at princely dwellings, Rilke hurried into books, when anguish flooded, and, like a dog hurrying after his master, who enters the house through the back door, he felt himself free.
He called ordinary existence life unlived.
Became that transient bird flown too far beyond the night.
Saddened by Paris, he dreamed of heating his room with pure mountain wood.
He longed to be a happy poet housed near peaks.
From his letters, words flow into darkness, the ceiling lowers, the air turns icy, the passage narrows—no light or sound, the current flows beneath impassable slabs.
An underground river, Rilke then dares the voyage few of us will take, risks everything anew.
Solemn as a priest he embraces the earth's heart, believes in her grace, sees with a hard eye.
These are his apostle days,
With melodies strong as ropes.
Sundays he also descends the steps of a cathedral, face grave, bereft of the terrifying angel, to settle deeper into prayer.
High on Raron's graveyard, the mountains have bedded him under blue skirts of ice.
What do my thoughts say when the image quarries lie empty, the word mines drowned?
Does God's idleness trap me too?
From the mirror an abandoned saint scrutinizes me.
Or do I stand alone in semi-darkness backstage while a symphony plays, seeing each musician's fingertips burn, hearing a myth being born?
Rilke wondered whether we can heed the star, wave or violin that waits for us.

We testify joyfully in the great void.
Marina Tsretaeva wrote: "You are not the poet I love most ...
You are poetry itself."
Like Orpheus, Rilke turns longing into praise.
The new music greets only this world.
On his epitaph *"Rose, oh pure contradiction, joy of being
No-one's sleep under so many lids,"* simple things find
their voice.
I wanted to remain on that Swiss slope, in that alpine cemetery—huge clouds giving us wings.
But when we reviewed our lives, the sky spoke with sleet,
Below us a train whistled.

Château

Wide open doors, this once. Rooms we divine,
rooms and the stories guests told.
An illusion of flight like those airy cathedrals,
erected for a God already withdrawn,
that rise with the earnest flair of some exalted angel
and were dismissed as "masterpieces of bad taste" by
vandals building lay dwellings with their stones. Today
this château—with its deserted stables—is open, and
in these oblivious times, prying for ancestors
is almost mystical; on old estates the past becomes
a sacred vessel, lures us into treasure hunts.
We too wandered through the château. No other
visitors around. Even the uniformed guards
invisible. High noon poppy hot. And we
spied the countess through a door. She didn't
feel the sun's needles through leaded glass window panes,
stood amidst paintings, virgin in a forest before the Unicorn,
finger posed on a portrait's peeling gold.
And expected perhaps an ancestor's glance to vaccinate.
We strained to hear her nails tapping
on the cracked canvas. The countess bent forward,
bent close, placing a kiss on the painted head.
And when she turned to leave she gave
the figure a final glance. The past she
released and held, softly, as a lover's face.

10 “All Saints”, the Catholic holiday when family graves are blessed and families often have reunion feasts.

21-22 “Immigrant” and “Only an Italian” commemorate the Italian labourers who immigrated to Esch, Luxembourg’s capital of iron and steel, at the beginning of the twentieth century. They formed the original backbone of Luxembourg’s prosperity today.

58 Nico Klopp (1894-1930), a notable Luxembourg landscape painter.

59 *46, rue Hippolyte-Maindron*, Giacometti had a modest studio for forty years at this street address in Paris. The quotation is drawn from Giacometti’s introduction to his book of lithographs *Paris without End*, 1964.

60 “The Cat” responds to the sculpture by that name and to Giacometti’s statements about cats.

61 “Nude with Head” was inspired by Giacometti’s painting *Head and Nude*, 1965.

62 *Lotar Seated III*, 1965, Giacometti’s last sculpture, modelled on the Parisian photographer Élie Lotar. This work is presently in the Museum at Stampa, the artist’s home village in Switzerland.

63 Talking to Jean Genet about *The Dog*, 1951, Giacometti is said to have made the statement in italics about this sculpture.

Critics on *Dream Museum*

"Welch paints her people and places with a palette of primary colours enriched with the noble elements of compassion, perception and brush work informed by a real concern for the cultural and the natural environment."

—E. Russel Smith, *The Pottersfield Portfolio*

"... a modern odyssey, *Dream Museum* orchestrates all the themes of human travel with a fierce passion for the infinite theatre of life."

—Anna Foschi, *L'Eco D'Italia*

"*Dream Museum* is a special event. To recite its lines is to be made "whole again" like the climber who reaches the challenge of the mountain peak."

—Michael O. Nowlan, *The Daily Gleaner*

"Welch's always original, precise imagery and her wonderful capacity to imagine other realities and possibilities imbue the work with clarity and energy, invite us to expand our field of vision."

—Maria Kubacki, *The New Brunswick Reader*

"...a sparkling blend of wit, sensuality, scepticism."

—Anna Greenwood, *The Argosy*

"The poems weave the reader into their rich tapestries, surrounding one with fascinating textures and colours."

—Sheila Martindale, *Scene*

About The Author

Liliane Welch has written fourteen collections of poetry, including *Life in Another Language*, which won the Bressani Prize. She has co-authored two volumes of literary criticism on modern French poetry, and has published a book of essays, *Seismographs*. Her writings have been widely anthologized and translated into French, German and Italian. Her many honours include the Alfred Bailey Prize. Liliane Welch teaches at Mount Allison University in Sackville, New Brunswick, Canada.

• Cap-Saint-Ignace
• Sainte-Marie (Beauce)
Québec, Canada
1997